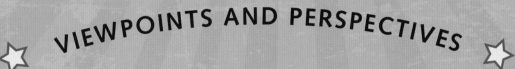

VIEWPOINTS ON
THE ATTACK ON
PEARL HARBOR

★ PART OF THE PERSPECTIVES LIBRARY ★

KRISTIN J. RUSSO

Published in the United States of America by Cherry Lake Publishing
Ann Arbor, Michigan
www.cherrylakepublishing.com

Reading Adviser: Marla Conn MS, Ed., Literacy specialist, Read-Ability, Inc.

Photo Credits: ©Lisa-Blue/Getty Images, cover (left); ©Samuel J. Hood Studio Collection/Wikimedia,
cover (middle); ©Wikimedia; cover (right); ©Lisa-Blue/Getty Images, 1 (left); ©Samuel J. Hood Studio
Collection/Wikimedia, 1 (middle); ©U.S. Navy/Wikimedia, 1 (right); ©Lisa-Blue/Getty Images, 4;
©David Franzen/Wikimedia, 7; ©Everett Collection/Newscom, 9; ©Joseph Sohm Visions of America/
Newscom, 11; ©Getty Images; 12; ©Uppa/Photoshot/Avalon via ZUMA Press/Newscom, 14; ©U.S. Naval
History and Heritage Command/Wikimedia, 16; ©UPPA/Photoshot/Newscom, 17; ©Samuel J. Hood
Studio Collection/Wikimedia, 18; ©Yoshino Collection/Wikimedia, 19; ©Everett Collection/Newscom,
21; ©Kent Nishimura/Getty Images, 22; ©Pictures From History/Newscom, 25; ©Shizuo Fukui/
Wikimedia, 29; ©U.S. Navy/Wikimedia, 31; ©U.S. Navy/Wikimedia, 32; ©Harold Fawcett, U.S. Navy/
Wikimedia, 35; ©US National Archives/Wikimedia, 36; ©Danita Delimont Photography/Newscom, 38;
©U.S. Navy/Wikimedia, 42; ©U.S. Navy/Wikimedia, 44; ©U.S. Navy/Wikimedia, 45; ©Abbie Rowe/
Wikimedia, 45

Library of Congress Cataloging-in-Publication Data has been filed and is available at catalog.loc.gov

Cherry Lake Publishing would like to acknowledge the work of The Partnership for 21st Century
Learning.
Please visit *www.p21.org* for more information.

Printed in the United States of America
Corporate Graphics

TABLE OF CONTENTS

In this book, you will read about the attack on Pearl Harbor from three perspectives. Each perspective is based on real things that happened to real people who were in or near the attack. As you'll see, the same event can look different depending on one's point of view.

MIRIAM HOP

WIFE OF HARVEY N. HOP,
A NAVY ENSIGN STATIONED AT PEARL HARBOR

I met Harvey in January 1941, on the beach at Waikiki. Two weeks later, we were married. Can you blame me? It was love at first sight for us both. He is a wonderful man, and so handsome! I told my friends, he is "six foot five and magnificent."

My parents have been so kind to let us stay with them in their quarters at Fort Kamehameha, the military base near Hickam

Field. My father is an Army warrant officer, and I have learned quite a bit from my mother, who lived the constantly changing life of a military wife. I am looking forward to the exciting adventures that being a military bride will bring.

THINK ABOUT IT

Read Miriam's description of life on a military base. Find sources that describe living on a military base today. How are they the same and different?

You would not think that Harvey and I have much in common—he is originally from Michigan, and I was born in Texas—but I feel like after almost a year of marriage, we are finally settling in to a happy domestic life. I was only 20 and Harvey 23 when we married. We have our whole lives ahead of us! Harvey loves his job as a Naval patrol-plane pilot, and we live a peaceful life in the tropical paradise that is the Hawaii Territory—at least we did until December 7, 1941.

It was a Sunday morning. Though he usually rises

SECOND SOURCE

Find a second source that describes what it was like to be witness to the attack on **Pearl Harbor**. Compare the information there to the information in this source.

early, a common military habit, Harvey chose to sleep late and ease into the day on that day. Do not get me wrong. Harvey is not lazy. He is an energetic and driven man. How could he not be? He has risen quickly through the military ranks. He joined the Naval Aviation Cadets in 1939 and became a full-fledged pilot in 1940. Soon after, he was assigned to the flying **squadron** right here in Pearl Harbor in the Territory of Hawaii. Our lives were perfect.

Suddenly, we were both shaken by a sound that could only be an explosion. We looked at each other. I tried to stay calm, thinking it may just be a drill, but Harvey moved quickly to look out the window. I knew something was terribly wrong when Harvey called my name in a way that alarmed me. It was both urgent

FORT KAMEHAMEHA, NAMED FOR A HAWAIIAN KING, WAS
LOCATED ON THE EAST SIDE OF THE ENTRANCE TO
PEARL HARBOR.

and calm at the same time. I asked him what was wrong. He told me he saw smoke coming from Hickam Field. He was right to be alarmed! This is

HITTING THE AIRFIELDS FIRST

Before bombing the ships anchored on Battleship Row, the Japanese hit U.S. military airfields on Ford Island. Many aircraft were destroyed when they were sitting on the airfields, unaware that the attack was coming. It was an attempt by the Japanese to prevent an American counterattack to protect the ships. But most of the aircraft were away from the harbor at that time. The aircraft that were not destroyed would be incredibly important to the United States' effort in the war. After attacking the airfields, the Japanese launched their attack on the battleships.

ON THE DAY OF THE ATTACK, 51 AIRPLANES WERE
ON THE GROUND AT HICKAM AIRFIELD. HALF WERE
DESTROYED OR SEVERELY DAMAGED.

where fighter planes and fuel tanks are stored. A fire at Hickam Field would be a disaster.

Harvey wondered aloud if the planes were being **sabotaged**. Great plumes of smoke filled the sky and explosions shook our house. Our quarters were only a half-mile away from Hickam airfield and 3 miles (5 kilometers) from Pearl Harbor. Harvey told me he saw smoke billowing from the harbor. The smoke and explosions can only mean one thing—an air strike! But by whom?

I rushed to join Harvey at the window, and he pointed out the **insignias** on the wings of the aircraft swarming overhead. They are "meatballs," he said, referring to their red color and circular shape. This means that the aircraft are Japanese planes, he explained. The red circles are also on the Japanese flag. They are the insignia of the land of the rising sun. It was clear to us. We were under attack.

Suddenly, we saw something that horrified us so

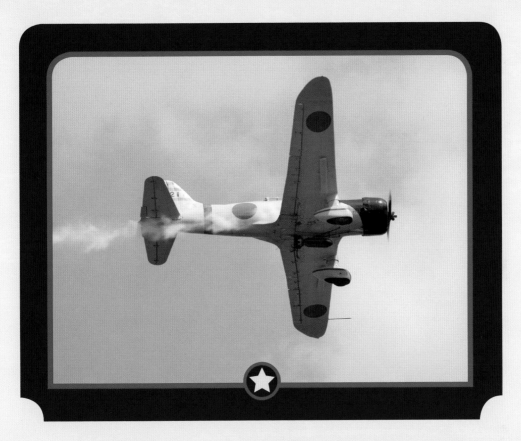

TWENTY-NINE JAPANESE AIRCRAFT WERE SHOT DOWN BY DEFENDING U.S. FORCES DURING THE ATTACK ON PEARL HARBOR.

badly that we ran out of our quarters and onto the street. A Japanese plane hit a U.S. plane. The Japanese pilot was flying so low we could see his aviator goggles. As the U.S. aircraft went up in flames, the Japanese pilot attempted to restart his stalled plane. Enraged, I screamed at Harvey, "Go kill him! Go kill

AFTER THE USS *WEST VIRGINIA* SANK, THE USS *TENNESSEE*, WHICH WAS MOORED TIGHTLY BESIDE HER, HAD TO BE BLASTED FREE.

him!" I think we were both surprised at my reaction, but to be surrounded by such violence is not something I had ever experienced before, not in all my years as the daughter of an Army officer.

Though Harvey had quickly **donned** his uniform so that he could report to his squadron, we both knew that he would never make it to his plane in time to give chase to the Japanese pilot. Of course, I knew that. I was just so overcome. Later, we learned that the plane was able to restart, and it crashed into a supply building a block away from the airfield. That pilot killed several U.S. soldiers in the building who were too shocked by the **chaos** to run for their lives.

With Japanese bombers swarming overhead, Harvey knew that he had to leave me and report for duty at the harbor's seaplane base. My mother and I volunteered to help the injured at the Hickam airfield hospital, and for the next three days, I heard nothing from Harvey. I was heartsick, unsure if harm had

SHIPS MOORED IN BATTLESHIP ROW WERE MOORED
TOGETHER SO TIGHTLY THAT DAMAGE FROM ONE SHIP
OFTEN SPREAD TO ANOTHER.

come his way.

What at first we thought was sabotage solely on
the fuel storage tanks and U.S. aircraft at Hickam Field
turned out to be a much more extensive assault. The
growing smoke plumes and **relentless** bombing at the

harbor told us so. But at this point, we had no idea how bad the situation was. It wasn't until much later, when the smoke finally cleared, that Harvey and I learned more about what we had witnessed. The bombing took the lives of more than 2,300 U.S. citizens.

More than 2,000 military personnel were lost, including 2,008 Navy sailors, 109 Marines, and 218 Army soldiers. Sadly, 68 civilians were also killed. More than 1,000 dead were sailors stationed aboard the USS *Arizona*, which was completely destroyed. Among those wounded were 710 Navy sailors, 69 Marines, and 364 Army soldiers. There were 103 civilians injured. Compared to U.S. deaths and casualties, at least 55 Japanese military personnel were lost.

The loss of human life was devastating, and the damage and loss of military artillery was just as shocking. Along with the USS *Arizona*, the USS

BEFORE ITS TRAGIC SINKING AT PEARL HARBOR, THE USS *ARIZONA* WAS KNOWN FOR PROVIDING HUMANITARIAN RELIEF.

Oklahoma was also destroyed. Twelve ships were sunk and nine others gravely damaged. In addition, 160 aircraft were destroyed and 150 more planes were damaged. It is hard to believe the surprise attack could do so much damage in only 2 hours.

I am so grateful to still have my husband beside me. My heart breaks for the loved ones of those who will never return home.

THE USS *WEST VIRGINIA* SUNK DURING THE ATTACK. LATER, THE SHIP WAS RAISED, AND AFTER A MAJOR RENOVATION, IT WAS BROUGHT BACK INTO SERVICE IN 1944.

2

TAKESHI MAEDA

IMPERIAL JAPANESE NAVY NAVIGATOR

I was only 17 years old, but I felt like I was old enough, I felt ready. In 1938, I joined the Imperial Japanese Navy. We had been at war with China for about a year at that point, and I felt it was my obligation to support my country. To receive, one must also give. I cannot accept the protection of my nation's military without also being willing to serve. I have always been interested in airplanes and the mechanics of flying, and I was pleased when I was assigned to work in aviation. I would have worked anywhere in the service of my country, but aviation is the best fit for me.

THE KAGA, JAPAN'S FIRST HEAVY AIRCRAFT CARRIER, WAS CONVERTED FROM A SMALLER BATTLESHIP. WHEN IT WAS COMPLETED IN 1928, THE CARRIER COULD HOLD A CREW OF 2,016.

It is important that you know that we did not want this war with the United States. Emperor Hirohito and his diplomats worked very hard to avoid it. But after the Great War, Japan was in a difficult position. We had little access to important resources, such as oil and rubber. We had to increase our influence over other countries in Asia, such as China, or we would have been too vulnerable. The emperor has to make sure he can provide for the people of Japan. It is my duty to serve and to help him reach that goal.

The United States did not approve of the emperor's plan to expand Japanese rule in Asia. The United States interfered and placed economic **sanctions** and trade **embargoes** on our small island nation. This angered Emperor Hirohito, though he continued to try to resolve problems with negotiations rather than war. Sadly, that did not work. We had no choice but to attack.

To protect themselves from the emperor's rightful displeasure, the U.S. military officials began to strengthen their military presence in the Pacific Ocean. This is just what we wanted! When more U.S. military battleships and aircraft were sent to Pearl Harbor, we saw this two ways. First, it was an

EMPEROR HIROHITO RELIED ON HIS WAR MINISTER LT. GENERAL HIDEKI TOJO TO CARRY OUT THE ATTACK ON PEARL HARBOR.

JAPANESE OFFICIALS SURRENDERED ABOARD THE
USS *MISSOURI* ON SEPTEMBER 2, 1945 IN TOKYO
BAY. U.S. GENERAL DOUGLAS MACARTHUR
ACCEPTED THE SURRENDER ON BEHALF OF ALL THE
ALLIED FORCES.

aggressive move. It meant that the United States expected war. Also, it meant that if we did engage in war, we had the perfect strategy: bomb the U.S. arsenal buildup and cripple the U.S. military all at once.

After years of negotiating, it finally became clear that the United States and Japan would not be able to solve their differences with **diplomatic** talk and peace

SECOND SOURCE

Find another source that discusses the embargo that the United States placed on Japan prior to the attack on Pearl Harbor. Compare the information here to the information in that source.

treaties. For one thing, not only has the United States enacted an oil embargo, it has persuaded its European allies to withhold oil and other resources from us as well! We are a small island nation, and we import 90 percent of our oil. Japanese people are hurting from these embargoes. This is just what the emperor feared, that Japan would become vulnerable. The emperor feels that a military response is the only answer to the

United States' unjust interference.

Since war is now inevitable, the emperor thinks it the best strategy for Japan to strike first. This is a new and different approach for us. During the Great War, and in the years following, our strategy was one of defense. This may be why U.S. officials did not expect Japan to launch an offensive assault. But we are different now. We are brave. We will not be trifled with. The United States will learn this soon enough.

The emperor has decided wisely that Japan should control regions that are rich in natural resources, so we will no longer be vulnerable to oil embargoes and other sanctions. Manchuria in China is just such a place. The United States wants us to leave China alone, but we cannot. That would not be a sound strategy for Japan. That is why it is important for us to be successful at Pearl Harbor. If we cannot destroy the U.S. military quickly, we will be vulnerable to counterattacks.

OF THE ENORMOUS JAPANESE ARTILLERY FORCE THAT CARRIED OUT THE ATTACK ON PEARL HARBOR, ONLY ONE, A DESTROYER CALLED *USHIO*, SURVIVED THE WAR.

In early November 1941, the Japanese military purposefully misled U.S. officials into thinking that we were only planning defensive operations and had no plans to launch an offensive attack. They used what is called "radio chatter" to do this. Japanese radio operators knew that the United States was listening to their radio communications, and so their messages indicated that all was calm and that no attack was imminent. All the while, however, Admiral Isoroku Yamamoto planned a sneak attack. This attack would take place at Pearl Harbor in the U.S. Hawaii Territory.

This plan was a most secretive plan. In fact, the radio chatter convinced U.S. **intelligence** that the Japanese aircraft carriers and submarines were far away in Japanese waters, even as they gathered closer and closer to the Hawaiian shores. Japanese submarines began moving closer to Pearl Harbor in Hawaii Territory on November 16, 1941. Aircraft carriers carrying more than 400 aircraft left for Hawaii on November 26.

While Japanese military personnel misled U.S. radio intelligence, they also developed radio intelligence of their own. They gathered information that told them where and when key U.S. ships and aircraft would be in the harbor or stored at nearby airfields. Tokyo merchant ships were also used to track U.S. fleet activity and report back to Japanese military intelligence.

Though U.S. officials did not know our plans, they had a sense that diplomatic talks were not going well. As a result, President Franklin Delano Roosevelt ordered more aircraft and more aircraft carriers to protect the U.S. Pacific Coast. This is exactly what we wanted! The more military equipment stored at Pearl Harbor, the more we could destroy.

We were jittery on the morning of December 7, 1941, which was December 8 on our side of the international dateline. We were not so tense, however, that we did not eat a full breakfast of red beans with rice and grilled fish. We even prayed before a Shinto shrine below deck before the mission. Our superior officers assured us that the U.S. forces did not suspect even for a minute that a surprise attack was on its way. This gave us courage and eased our anxiety.

I was assigned to the aircraft carrier *Kaga* and was the pilot of a torpedo bomber. The aircraft carriers were about 300 miles (500 km) north of Hawaii.

When we received orders to carry out the attack, I knew this meant that we were at war with the United States.

I took off from the aircraft carrier at about 6:05 in the morning. It took less than 2 hours to reach our target. By 7:55 in the morning, we had begun our attack. Submarines torpedoed U.S. battleships from below and high-level bombers dropped bombs from 20,000 feet (6,000 meters) above the harbor in the first wave. Later, I swooped low, and my crew fired. In all,

BELIEVED TO BE AT WAR

When the Japanese attacked Pearl Harbor, most Japanese pilots believed their country was already at war with the United States. Striking an enemy before war is declared is against Japanese cultural values and customs.

THE JAPANESE AIRCRAFT CARRIER *KAGA* PLAYED A MAJOR ROLE IN THE ATTACK ON PEARL HARBOR. IT WAS LATER SUNK BY U.S. AIRCRAFT AT THE BATTLE OF MIDWAY ON JUNE 4, 1942.

ANALYZE THIS

Analyze this account of the attack on Pearl Harbor. How is it different from the account by the U.S. naval pilot's wife? How is it similar?

seven torpedoes, some from aircraft and some from submarines below the water's surface, hit the USS *West Virginia*, killing 106 sailors on board.

There was no resistance at all from U.S. military forces. I knew when I heard, "Tora, tora, tora!" over my radio that we had surprised our target. Tora means "tiger" in Japanese, and it was the code word indicating that we had succeeded in the element of surprise. U.S. warships moored in the harbor had no time to retaliate. U.S. soldiers and sailors were taken completely by surprise. Later, we learned it was the same for pilots involved in the assault on Hickam airfield. Once the torpedo bombers released their bombs, there was no chance for the United States to rally a counterattack. It grieved me to cause this loss of life, but I had my orders, and I had to

EIGHT U.S. NAVY BATTLESHIPS WERE MOORED AT WHAT WAS KNOWN AS BATTLESHIP ROW WHEN THE ATTACK BEGAN. SOME SHIPS WERE LOST COMPLETELY, WHILE OTHERS WERE REPAIRED AND BROUGHT BACK INTO SERVICE LATER IN THE WAR.

follow them.

A few U.S. artillerymen were able to reach and shoot some of our pilots, and we lost at least 55 men. I grieve those losses as well, but they died in the service of their nation. They died an honorable death.

ROBERT VARILL

U.S. NAVY FIREMAN

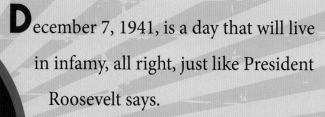

December 7, 1941, is a day that will live in infamy, all right, just like President Roosevelt says.

It was a Sunday morning and all we wanted was to take it easy. There was no sign that we had anything to worry about. The sky was blue, the weather was clear; it was going to be a good day. We were just going about our business when all of a sudden, the sky fell in.

I do not mean that literally, of course, but that is what it felt like. The bombs fell from airplanes overhead, and the torpedoes hit us from submarines underneath. No matter which way we turned, we were under attack. There was no escape, and the focus was not about fighting back, not right away at least. All that mattered was to survive. So many of us did not.

I was just a 20-year-old Navy fireman thrilled to be stationed in Hawaii Territory. It was paradise compared to the New Hampshire winters that I was used to. I was out on the USS *Sunnadin*, a tugboat, when the bombs started falling. At first we all thought it was a drill, but pretty soon we figured out the whole thing was all too real.

Later, when I was questioned by a reporter, it was painful to recall what had happened. I told him, "Bombers from overhead roared down toward the battleships, and before we knew it, the *Oklahoma* rolled over and the *Arizona* exploded. There was no question then that this was a real attack!"

My shipmate, John Frank Lynch, and I ran to our battle station and set off in a 26-foot (8-m) motorized whaleboat—not very big, but good for making our way quickly through and around obstacles in the water. The two of us pulled as many injured and drowning men as we could from the harbor.

Oil escaping from the downed ships spilled into the harbor and spread on the surface. The smell was overpowering, but we didn't let anything stop us. As soon as we delivered a boat full of survivors to crew waiting to help them on the docks, we headed back out again for more. The men we picked up did not look too good. Many looked like they would not make it, their injuries were so bad, but as far as I know, John and I did not lose any of the men we ferried to safety on the docks. We

ANALYZE THIS

How is the perspective of the attack from a naval pilot's point of view different than from a civilian's point of view? How are they similar?

BOTH THE USS *DOWNES* AND THE USS *CASSIN* WERE IN DRYDOCK BEING RENOVATED WHEN THE ATTACK OCCURRED. NEITHER SHIP COULD FIRE BACK RIGHT AWAY BECAUSE THEIR GUNS HAD BEEN DISMANTLED.

saved about two dozen men. I am proud of that.

By the end of the day, John and I were covered with oil. Our shipmates used diesel fuel to help us scrub the oil off. It is something I will never forget. The next day, we headed back out on the motorboat looking for survivors. Sadly, by this time, we only found corpses.

MANY FORMER MEMBERS OF THE *ARIZONA* CREW WHO SURVIVED THE ATTACK LATER ASKED TO HAVE THEIR REMAINS "BURIED" WITH THEIR CREWMATES AT THE SITE OF THE SINKING.

We did not panic though. What good would that do? There was no place for panic either during the attack or in the aftermath. All I felt was anger. I was mad. Still am, to be honest. For so many, it's just a heartbreaking disaster. Take John Grand Pre, for example. John and his brother, Art, those two were inseparable. When Art joined the Navy, John did too. They were the closest brothers I have ever met. From South Dakota, I think they were. Anyway, they were assigned to the boiler rooms on the *Oklahoma*. When the bombing started, they both jumped into the harbor, trying to escape the bombs and the flames. John swam to the *Maryland*. At first he thought his brother was safe, but he was wrong. Art had been shot by Japanese strafing while he was in the water.

And the Marines with us at Pearl Harbor took it

THINK ABOUT IT

Determine the main point of this paragraph. Pick out one piece of evidence that supports the main point.

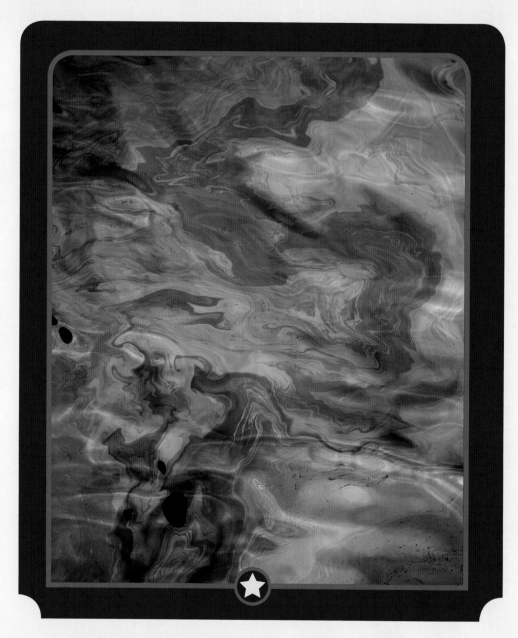

THE DAY BEFORE THE ATTACK, THE USS *ARIZONA* LOADED UP WITH NEARLY 1.5 MILLION GALLONS OF FUEL. CALLED "THE TEARS OF THE *ARIZONA*, THAT FUEL STILL LEAKS INTO THE WATER TODAY.

just as bad. Let me tell you about Marine Corporal E.C. Nightingale. He was stationed aboard the USS *Arizona*. The *Arizona* was moored with all the other ships along Battleship Row. This was the Japanese bombers' target in the first wave of the attack.

The Japanese got a lucky hit on the *Arizona*'s ammunition room. When the artillery ignited, it ripped a hole in the side of the ship. The *Arizona* went down in minutes. More than 1,000 members of its crew were killed by the sinking or by artillery fire. By some turn of luck, Nightingale survived.

Nightingale reported that at about 8 o'clock in the morning, an air defense siren sounded. Since his battle station was not anti-aircraft, he did not pay as much attention to it as maybe he should have. After he heard an explosion, he got serious real quick. He ran for the quarterdeck, and just as he reached it, he saw a bomb strike a barge that was next to the *Nevada*. He knew then that we were under attack!

Nightingale said he then ran to Major Shapley to report some details of the attack that he had witnessed. They were together when the *Arizona* was ripped apart by exploding artillery. He said Major Shapley ordered everyone to abandon ship.

Nightingale really had no choice about it. He said

MEMORIALS

Pearl Harbor is now home to many memorials and museums that honor those who died during the attack. The most well-known memorial is the USS *Arizona* Memorial, which is formally called the World War II Valor in the Pacific National Monument. It consists of a 184-foot (56-m) structure built over the remains of the sunken battleship.

the concussion from a nearby bomb shook the *Arizona* so badly that he was thrown into the water. Surrounded by drowning and injured sailors, he was just the man we were looking for—survivors amid the chaos. But Nightingale did not need Lynch and me to help him. Major Shapley was still near. He saw Nightingale nearly succumb to fatigue and shock, and he helped Nightingale swim to safety.

Nightingale and Shapley were among those who survived the sinking of the *Arizona*. They both made it to a bomb shelter where they were given dry clothes and a chance to rest.

It was not until later that we learned what was going on. I mean, we could tell it was the Japanese that was after us by the round, red circle insignias on their aircraft wings. We call them "meatballs," if I'm being honest about it. But we had to wait to get the full story from the president on the radio. President Roosevelt announced that December 7, 1941 is "a date which

JAPANESE BOMBERS ATTACKED PEARL HARBOR IN TWO
WAVES. B5N2 BOMBERS ATTACKED IN THE FIRST WAVE
AND AICHI D3A1 DIVE BOMBERS WERE USED IN THE
SECOND WAVE.

will live in infamy." This is due to the devastating

surprise attack we suffered at the hands of the

Japanese Imperial Navy on that day.

Japanese aviators began their flight to Pearl

Harbor at about 6:00 a.m., and the first bombs fell at about 8:00 a.m. Since the attack took place so early in the morning, the U.S. Navy sailors and Marines stationed at Pearl Harbor, John and I among them, were taken completely by surprise.

The first bombs were dropped on aircraft parked in hangars at Hickam Field. By the time the attack was more than 2 hours later, 12 ships and 9 others were heavily damaged, 160 aircraft were destroyed and 150 more were damaged, and more than 2,300 American service men and women were killed.

Not surprisingly, on December 8, the United States declared war on Japan. Not long after, nations that were friendly with Japan, Germany and Italy, declared war on the United States. As a result, the United States joined the allied forces of Great Britain, France, and Russia in the fight against Germany and Italy in Europe in World War II. There is no doubt that this is going to get uglier before it gets better.

TIMELINE

ATTACK ON PEARL HARBOR

The United States imposes an oil embargo and other trade sanctions against Japan in an effort to stop Japan's aggression in China and other areas of Asia.

JULY
1940

Admiral Yamamoto recommends planning a surprise assault on the United States at Pearl Harbor in Hawaii Territory. U.S. officials become aware of a possible attack, but few believe it because the Japanese have never committed this type of assault.

JANUARY
1941

Submarines leave Japan and head toward Hawaii Territory.

NOVEMBER 16,
1941

NOVEMBER 26,
1941

Japanese aircraft carriers and escorts begin moving toward Hawaii Territory.

DECEMBER 7,
1941

At 7:55 a.m. Hawaiian time, the attack on Pearl Harbor begins. The attack continues for more than 2 hours.

DECEMBER 8,
1941

President Roosevelt asks Congress to approve a declaration of war against Japan. Congress grants the approval.

Take a close look at this photo of Pearl Harbor and answer the following questions:

1. What would a civilian see in this picture? What would the wife of a U.S. aviator think when she saw Japanese planes flying overhead? Would she think of them as villains or heroes? Why?

2. What would a Japanese aviator see in this picture? How would he describe this scene to his friends and family back home in Japan?

3. What would a U.S. Navy sailor see in this picture? Would it be different from what the Japanese aviator sees? Why and how?

GLOSSARY

chaos *(KAY-oss)* disorder and confusion

diplomatic *(dip-lo-MA-tick)* negotiating in a tactful and sensitive way

donned *(DAWND)* put on something, such as an item of clothing or equipment

embargoes *(em-BAR-goes)* bans on trade or other commercial activities

insignias *(in-SIG-neeyaz)* official emblems

intelligence *(in-TEL-ih-jens)* information that has political or military value

Pearl Harbor *(PURL HAR-bur)* a U.S. Naval Base in Hawaii

relentless *(re-LENT-less)* continuous and nonstop

sabotaged *(SAB-uh-tajd)* destroyed or damaged something, especially to gain an advantage

sanctions *(SANK-shuns)* penalties for disobeying a rule

squadron *(SKWAH-drun)* a large group of aircraft and aviators

LEARN MORE

FURTHER READING

Bodden, Valerie. *The Attack on Pearl Harbor.* Mankato, MN: Creative Education, 2018.

Nobleman, Marc Tyler. *Thirty Minutes Over Oregon: A Japanese Pilot's World War II Story.* New York: Clarion Books, 2018.

Otfinoski, Steven. *The Split History of the Attack on Pearl Harbor.* North Mankato, MN: Compass Point Books, 2018.

WEBSITES

The Attack on Pearl Harbor

https://www.britannica.com/event/Pearl-Harbor-attack

This website describes what happened during the attack on Pearl Harbor.

Historic Site

http://www.pearlharborhistoricsites.org

This website explains the battle and will help you plan a visit to the historic site where the attack on Pearl Harbor took place.

INDEX

ABOUT THE AUTHOR

Kristin J. Russo is a university English lecturer. She loves teaching, reading, writing, and learning new things. She and her husband live near Providence, Rhode Island, in a small house surrounded by flower gardens. They have three grown children and three rescue dogs.